WILD ABOUT **BARNES**

The Village on the River

*For Diana, Sam and Amy (my family) and for their unshakable support for what I do
and not forgetting Josie of course*

FOREWORD

A great city is really a collection of urban villages, each with its own identity contributing to the overall charm and character of the metropolis. Barnes is one of London's most attractive villages, a community which stretches across and around woods and common land from the station to the banks of The Thames.

Its streets are lined by some of the most attractive houses in any city; no wonder most people don't ever want to leave once they have put down their roots here. Moreover, our village community has all the urban attributes which have not yet been obliterated by the onward march of shopping malls.

We have a great bookshop, staffed by people who love books and can tell you with authority what you should be reading. There's a great butcher ("morning, young man") who ensures that the Sunday joints in Barnes attract the whole family home for lunch. There's a terrific farmers' market every Saturday morning bringing fresh fish, great apples, seasonal vegetables, delicious onion tarts, bread and delicatessen treats to the spoilt-rotten residents.

There are busy churches and good pubs, including the Bull's Head where you can hear some of the best jazz in London over a pint. At the bottom of Castelnau, which joins the centre of Barnes to the rest of the world in transpontine London, there is the best Italian restaurant in the whole city. For dog-owners like me the walks are easy and many: from home past the pond and the ducks to the best newsagent in London for the Sunday papers; across to the cemetery and the fields beyond; up to the river and the tow-path to Hammersmith Bridge. Alas, the bird sanctuary at the Wetlands is no good for dogs but great for grand-children, especially if you buy a brownie for them in the café afterwards.

So, Barnes for me is not just where I sleep but where I live and want to live until closing time. I see no reason why it should ever change. Semper eadem, as the Chancellor of Oxford University might put it.

Lord Patten of Barnes

WELCOME TO THE WONDER OF **BARNES**

Welcome to my latest collection of pictures. My first two books were very much my own creation but I am pleased to say that they were the catalyst for this my latest work. Almost a year ago Isla Dawes, from Barnes Bookshop, and her partner Mark Brighton approached me and asked whether I would put together a new collection on Barnes. Several historical books have been produced but nothing modern.

Isla, having lit the touch paper, then inspired me set about the project, which I did with much relish. Living on the borders of Barnes as I do, I feel I know this area really well, which can of course be beneficial when wanting to know where to get the best vantage points for that perfect picture. However, what I found amazing was discovering how much I didn't know. For instance, I had never visited Barnes Bowls Club behind the Sun Inn. In fact I didn't know it was their. It was a brilliant excuse to visit places that I wouldn't normally go and in the course of doing so meet a wonderful new set of people.

This project has been a year in the making and terrific fun and I hope that when you are taking a look at my book that some of this magic drifts off the page for you too. To try and give the book some structure and to help you find your way, the content falls into neat sub-sections and if you study the contents list opposite I hope that this will be easy to follow. As with my previous books, I have included a simple map to help you place my pictures geographically and I am grateful to my brother, Jeremy Wilson, for again supplying this. Something new for this year, is being able to announce the setting up of the Barnes Trail, which is going to open early next year. This is a fantastic initiative and a huge boost for Barnes, so please take a look at what is being proposed. I know you will enjoy it.

As with all photographic assignments of this kind, it is never a one man show and there are numerous people to thank. Firstly, Isla Dawes and her partner Mark Brighton, whose idea it was.

Maisie Brown, our foremost local historian, for supplying not only an introduction but also a lot of captions. Thank you also to Maisie's husband, Monty, as it was he that persuaded Maisie to help me. Pretty much retired, this was some commitment on Maisie's part and I would like to take my hat off to them both for summoning up the energy to help me. Further, together with my wife, Maisie also helped proof the whole thing, which for a job of this length was a monumental task, so thank you.

I would like to thank Lord Patten, for providing such a wonderfully evocative foreword. I would also like to thank Gyles Brandreth, Isla Blair, Julian Glover and Patricia Hodge for taking time out of their busy schedules to give me a few lines on why they love Barnes so much. They have all done a splendid job and you can see their contributions spread out amongst the first 50 pages. May I also thank all the people whose 'property' I visited to take pictures, from Richmond Council who own much of it to the owner of Strawberry House, who kindly let me in to take an up-to-date picture. Finally, Simon Banks and all the staff at Charles Banks (our foremost local estate agents), who kindly agreed to sponsor me, which was brilliant of them. There is just not enough space to thank everybody but I hope you know that you are not forgotten and that when you see my book you will be pleased with how it's turned out.

As I say, this has been a huge undertaking but brilliant fun and I do hope you enjoy it.

Andrew Wilson, October 2011

Josie, my always happy 'assistant', even on the occasions that I ask her to sit still.

CONTENTS

BARNES - A SHORT HISTORY

Barnes is a small suburb of south-west London, lying on the south bank of the Thames, some six miles distant from Hyde Park Corner. The greater part of the land is a peninsula, bordered on three sides by a pronounced northern meander of the Thames. The terrain is almost uniformly flat, rising only 27ft above flood level at Mill Hill on Barnes Common. Barnes was once in the County of Surrey. On April 1st 1965 it became part of the Greater London Borough of Richmond upon Thames.

Long before the Norman Conquest in 1066, Barnes was a settled village within the Archbishop of Canterbury's Manor of Mortlake in the county of Surrey, together with Putney, Roehampton, Wimbledon and Mortlake itself. Early in the reign of the Anglo Saxon King Athelstan (925 - 939AD), Barnes became a separate manor held in Lordship by the Dean and Chapter of St. Paul's Cathedral, London. It was one of eighteen small manors within easy reach of London owned by the Cathedral Chapter and known collectively as the Communa. "The revenue and produce of which were appropriated to the support and sustenance of all members of the Cathedral in regular gradation…from the Dean down to the humblest servitor - the doorkeeper of the brewery." The manors were leased to a Firmarius, an office limited to resident canons which was a source of wealth. They in turn sub-let the manors to tenants who tended the soil and were required to send regular quantities of grain to the Cathedral - wheat, oats and barley - to make bread and beer. Most of the eighteen manors were in Middlesex; Barnes was the only one on the Surrey bank of the Thames.

In the Great Survey of England, ordered by William I in 1086, better known as the Domesday Book, Barnes is recorded as a settled pre-conquest Anglo Saxon village, "the land of St. Paul's, London", held by the Canons of St. Paul's. In 1086 the population numbered around 60 to 65. The manor appears to have been close to what used to be termed the 'classic manor', made up of land reserved for the lord of the manor, known as the *demesne* with the remainder shared equally among the village tenants. In Barnes the *demesne* amounted to 460 acres to the north of the village, later known as the Barn Elms Estate. The tenants shared the two arable fields, the Westfield and the Northfield, in equal lots, plus a limited amount of meadow for animal winter feed. In return they were obliged to work for three days in each week on the *demesne* plus payments in money or kind. No mention is made of the "waste" or Common, an invaluable resource for the tenants providing forage for their geese and pigs and fallen wood for fuel, but was probably considered not worth a mention by the Norman assessors as it was worth very little to the exchequer.

Barnes Parish Church, 1837 (from a lithograph by Laura Jones) - Barnes and Mortlake History Society

By the end of the 15th century, payment in kind had been commuted into money payment in Barnes. And in 1467, Sir John Saye, Chancellor to Edward IV, became the first of a long line of lay tenants who leased the Barn Elms Estate and possibly built the first Manor House, Barn Elms, in its grounds.

In 1579 Elizabeth I leased the Manor of Barnes and gave it to her spymaster-in-chief, Sir Francis Walsingham, who was there until his death in 1590. During his tenure the Queen is known to have visited Barn Elms on several occasions sometimes alone and at other times with her court. Living nearby at Milbourne House, was Robert Beale, secretary to Sir Francis and no doubt the vexed question of what to do about Mary, Queen of Scots was often discussed at Barn Elms. Beale was among the party who carried the order to Fotheringay for the execution of the unfortunate Queen and witnessed her beheading.

Walsingham, head of a network of domestic and foreign spies, probably appreciated the seclusion of the estate, accessible only by river and remote from the village which, due to the lack of a permanent river crossing, was itself a quiet and isolated place. However, the river Thames was a major highway carrying both goods and people, so that isolation was never total.

At the beginning of the 17th century, the pattern of open field farming in the Westfield and Northfield, laid down centuries before, was rapidly transformed into one of small individual enclosures. As peasant farmers responded to the demands of the growing London fruit and vegetable market they turned from cereal crops to market gardening. Each day river barges carrying garden produce were seen leaving Barnes bound for the newly opened Covent Garden Market. Civil War, when it came, left the market gardens undisturbed as no battles were fought in Barnes. It was the gardeners pockets which suffered. Between 1642 and 1645 heavy taxation imposed by the Parliamentarians, the commandeering of horses and food supplies and the billeting of soldiers on private households weighed heavily on all but the poorest in Barnes.

Towards the end of the century a period of slow recovery which began with the restoration of the Monarchy began to gather pace and the village entered into a period of mild prosperity. The population increased, as did the number of small traders and craftsmen. Shops and inns opened on the path between the two open fields, which was now known as 'the Streete'. Barnes even had its own 'garden centre' where William Blinde stocked rare plants, still relatively new to England, as well as the 'ordinarie sortes of flowers'.

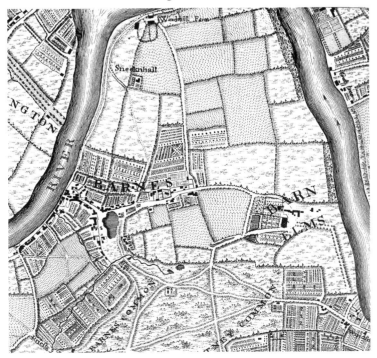

The larger scale portion of John Roques survey of London covering Barnes published 1746.

All this was largely due to the market garden trade with London. The market gardens were the backbone of the local economy in Barnes for the next 230 years. The last market gardener left in 1926.

When the first census was taken in 1801, Barnes had a population of 860. The 1838 Tithe Map of Barnes recorded a landscape consisting mostly of market gardens, farms and common land. The Manor House was at Barn Elms, there were a number of large houses along The Terrace and others stood in their own grounds around The Green and along Church Road. Some were leased as summer lets or for longer periods by well-to-do Londoners escaping from the unhealthy city. They contrasted sharply with the huddle of mean cottages crammed into the courts and alleys behind the High Street and The Terrace which housed the 'working classes', mostly migrants who came to work in the market gardens. One visitor described the cottages as closely resembling overcrowded pigsties.

For many years, wealthy families such as the merchant bankers, like the Hoares, who leased the Barn Elms estate from 1732 to 1824, favoured Barnes as a semi-rural retreat, conveniently within reach of their businesses in the City of London, and were content to preserve their peaceful surroundings by sub-letting their surplus land to market gardeners and farmers. When the suggestion of a bridge joining Hammersmith to Barnes was first raised in parliament in 1671 it had been greeted by laughter and cries of "why build a bridge to a place where nobody lives."

The first Hammersmith Bridge, depicting the Boat Race and spectators literally hanging off the bridge.

A proposal in 1817 by the newly formed Hammersmith Bridge Company to build a bridge providing the most direct way from London to the South West was taken more seriously.

A Bill authorising the building of the bridge, had little chance of being enacted in Parliament until the land for an approach road had been acquired and the only possible route was through the Barn Elms estate. Henry Hugh Hoare the lessee, was adamant. If the company wanted to build their road across his land they would have to buy the lease of the entire estate, which eventually they did, for £35,000. The enabling Bill was enacted on 9th June 1824 and the first Hammersmith Bridge designed by William Tierney Clark was opened on 6th October 1827. It was the first of the major changes destined to transform a quiet village into a suburb of London. The next was the coming of the railway in 1846, since when Barnes has slowly developed into the pleasant leafy place we know today.

Maisie Brown
Past Chairman of the Barnes and Mortlake History Society.

Barnes Bridge Circa 1849.

Barnes Pond - this is an original watercolour by Jeremy Wilson and produced exclusively for this book. A limited number of prints will be available after publication - please contact the publisher for more details.

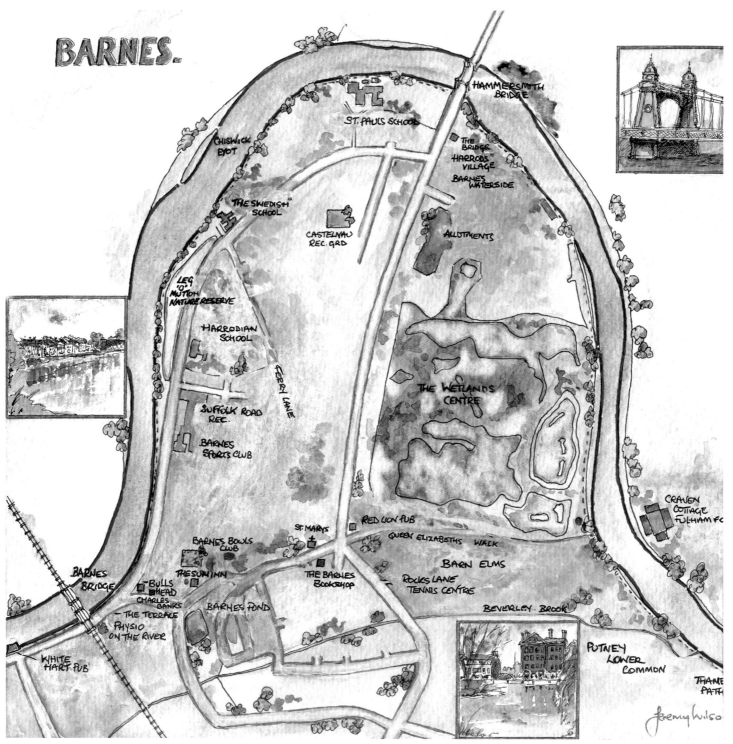

BARNES.

HAMMERSMITH BRIDGE

ST. PAULS SCHOOL

CHISWICK EYOT

THE BRIDGE

HARRODS VILLAGE

BARNES WATERSIDE

THE SWEDISH SCHOOL

CASTELNAU REC. GRD

ALLOTMENTS

LEG "O" MUTTON NATURE RESERVE

HARRODIAN SCHOOL

FERRY LANE

THE WETLANDS CENTRE

SUFFOLK ROAD REC.

BARNES SPORTS CLUB

CRAVEN COTTAGE FULHAM FC

RED LION PUB

ST. MARYS

QUEEN ELIZABETHS WALK

BARNES BOWLS CLUB

BARN ELMS

THE SUN INN

THE BARNES BOOKSHOP

ROCKS LANE TENNIS CENTRE

BARNES BRIDGE

BULLS HEAD
CHARLES BANKS

BEVERLEY BROOK

THE TERRACE

BARNES POND

PHYSIO ON THE RIVER

PUTNEY LOWER COMMON

WHITE HART PUB

THAMES PATH

Jeremy Wilson

This watercolour map, which has been produced especially for this publication is not meant
to be to scale but purely to act as a guide to Barnes and some of the places covered by this book.

10

THE POND AND GREEN
The Heart of the Village

The pond on Barnes Green has long been a local community focal point at the centre of Barnes Village. Known to generations of children as a place to feed the ducks and to Barnes people in general as somewhere to spare a moment to sit and watch the world go by. Just how long the pond has been there, nobody knows. Archival references are rare, one being a survey of the manor of Barnes in 1649, when it was named as The Great Pond, part of the glebe land belonging to the Rector of St. Mary's Parish Church, although its origins are thought to date back far earlier than the 17thC. Also mentioned in the survey were three smaller ponds on the Green. They lasted until the 19thC, during which they were drained at various times due to stagnation.

A serious threat to the pond came in 1824, when the Hammersmith Bridge Company published a plan to run a road across its centre as part of an approach road to their proposed bridge across the Thames. Thankfully the plan was abandoned. In April, 2001, early morning walkers on the Green were the first to be greeted by the amazing sight of the pond minus its water. No definitive cause was ever established. The local community, led by the Barnes Community Association together with Richmond Council, raised a substantial amount of money that enabled the pond to be 'repaired'; fitting for the first time in its long history an artificial liner.

The Pond and Green in winter.

"I am not sure that it's really a good idea to publish
a book about the beauty of Barnes. Those of us who are
lucky enough to live here don't necessarily want to spread the
word. But perhaps it's too late. It seems that Barnes has had
its admirers for centuries. Samuel Pepys loved Barnes.
According to his diary, he used to wander across Barn Elms,
watching the girls go by. Henry Fielding, the novelist and
magistrate, loved Barnes. He lived here. (I think there
should be a statue of him on the traffic island outside
his house by Barnes Pond.)"
**Gyles Brandreth - local resident, broadcaster,
writer and all round good egg.**

Beverley Brook

Picture Top: Methodists first came to Barnes in 1860 acting as missionaries to the gipsy families encamped on Barnes Common. They later held open air meetings on Barnes Green. A small chapel in White Hart Lane served as their base from 1867 until sufficient funds were raised to build the present church, known to many as 'the Church on the Green', at a cost of £6,000 in 1906.

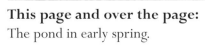

This page and over the page:
The pond in early spring.

15

The Green in autumn.

Top: The pond in spring.
Above and left: The Green has a beautiful display of Crocuses that bloom in February.

Left:
This square box-like structure on the side of Beverley Brook by the bridge to the common was placed there in 1960. It housed a pump which sent water from the brook to the pond via an underground pipe across the Green. By the early 1970's the pipe was found to be ineffective, since when no water from the brook has entered the pond.

Left: The houses beside the Green after a particularly heavy summer shower.
Below: The Barnes Green Centre that houses the voluntary group FiSH, which provides help in the community as well as a day centre for the elderly.

"I moved to Barnes in 1968 and cannot imagine living anywhere else. It is the last remaining 'village' in London with a wonderful community spirit. There are many and varied societies and organisations and I shop locally, not just in support, but because the local shops are so good. There is a thriving WI, Farmer's Market and a vibrant Literary Society and Music and Drama Society. I travel a great deal but each time I cross Hammersmith Bridge I sigh and say - Ah, Barnes - because coming home here is the best feeling one could have."

Isla Blair, novelist Oct 2011

Feeding the pigeons

Left: A sight you don't see so often these days - an old fashioned boat on a string on the pond.
Below: a rather more modern form of kids entertainment spotted on the Green.

Far right and middle left: Each summer the geese are rounded up and their health checked.

Right: A mother Mallard and her ducklings.

Bottom right: A Canada goose keeping a special eye on her goslings.

Mallard duckling.

Above right: Unfortunately, the Green has many Horse Chestnut trees which are slowly being killed by moths, that each year weaken them by eating the chlorophyll in their leaves. That's why they are prematurely dropping them, as if autumn has arrived in August. As can be seen, one has already been cut back leaving just a stump. If this carries on, the Green will start to look very sad.
Opposite Page: An 'aerial' shot of the pond. Thank you to the staff of Rodgers & Burton, solicitors, for allowing me to take this picture and the one on page 87 from one of their office windows.

The Lion Houses are a major feature of the homes that surround the Green and were built by a local builder, James or Jimmy Nicholls, between 1899 and 1903. Nicholls' building yard was at the end of Willow Avenue, known as Beverley Works. The first to be built were Nos. 1 to 14 The Crescent, followed by others in Laurel Road, Hillersdon Avenue and Glebe Road. An attractive and unusual feature of the houses, much prized by their owners, is the small sandstone lions that peer down at passers-by from every vantage point. It is said that their widespread use was due to 1,000 lions being supplied by mistake for the 100 ordered by the builder.

Another feature of the Green is the annual ***Barnes Fair***, which normally takes place on the second Saturday in July. One of the biggest in London, it regularly attracts over 10,000 people. Besides the many stalls that cover both sides of the Green, there is also a procession with floats through the streets led by some of the local school children.

Above left: In 2011 a company were letting people try out Paddle Surfing, which was very popular.
Left: Laying out the tables the day before.

Top: The Brown Dog brought their fabulous burgers to the pond and delicious they were too.
Above left: The procession as it passed Strada and The Bull's Head.
Right: The procession in 2011 included some vintage cars.

THE RIVER AND TERRACE

The Terrace is a row of highly individual riverside dwellings, mostly residential, running west from the end of Barnes High Street to White Hart Lane. The larger houses mostly date from the early to mid-18thC. Some of the smaller houses that are thought to have started out as watermen's cottages, may be considerably older, possibly dating from the 16th century. They would have been among the earliest buildings to appear on the riverside boundary of the Westfield, one of the two medieval open fields of Barnes. During the 18th and 19th century the larger houses were popular as summer lets, especially to wealthy Londoners making their escape from the overcrowded and unhealthy city.

Some houses no longer exist. Several made way for Barnes Railway Bridge in 1849, its widening in 1895 and for Barnes Bridge Station in 1916. And slightly further to the west the largest and most imposing house on The Terrace, Elm Bank, lost 5 acres of its land to Elm Bank Gardens in 1896. The house itself disappeared to make way for Elm Bank Mansions built in 1906 (see page 50). Only the entrance to the carriage driveway, marked by two decorative pillars, and the Tower, a folly which stood in its grounds, still stands, the latter as part of Tower House (see page 48). River House, an apartment block, was built in 1963 on the former site of Nos 18-24. More recently, a prominent feature of The Terrace, a malthouse dating from the 18thC, was demolished to make way for Numbers 1-4 Maltings Close, a residential development which somewhat surprisingly stands with its back to the riverside view. But happily several old houses and cottages still stand, looking outwardly much the same as in old prints of The Terrace and lending a touch of bygone elegance to the riverside scene.

The big Moon we had in the spring of 2011, as it rose up over the High Street.

"During the 45 years that I have lived in Barnes it has never occurred to
me to go elsewhere. It is leafy, it is attractive and it has shops which are so good,
people from other areas visit them. It is wonderfully easy to get to the heart of
London and out again. Every time I walk its streets I meet someone I know
(and usually like!). It is cosy. Why would I want to move?"

Julian Glover, actor Oct 2011

Left and on the page opposite: Two of the more famous residents of The Terrace have had their houses marked with Blue Plaques: Gustav Holst, the composer and Dame Ninette de Valois, the founder of the Royal Ballet.

Top right, right and far right:
In the spring one of the houses has
a spectacular display of Wisteria.

Malthouse Passage is one of the many footpaths to be found across Barnes and runs next to Barnes Bridge Station.

Above: The High Street as it meets The Terrace, with Strada on the corner of Lonsdale Road and The Bull's Head in the background.

"Ah! Barnes. For me it was love at first sight.
Green and leafy, with low-rise houses, a flowing
waterside and a wetland centre, a vast common, a brook,
a duck pond and a quaintness that's the nearest
approximation to the Lincolnshire villages
of my childhood yet within 20 minutes of Piccadilly
Circus (if you erase the traffic)…The perfect hybrid
between London and the country. After 36 years here,
I think one could say the love affair is enduring".

Patricia Hodge - actress Oct 2011

Elm Bank Mansions
on the left and
River House.

The new display along the riverside promoting the wildlife of The Wetland Centre.

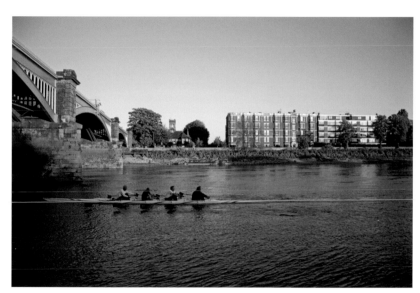

Looking west towards Mortlake and the Brewery from Ye White Hart.

THE RIVER

Looking east towards Chiswick, with The Leg o' Mutton Nature Reserve behind the trees on the right of the river.

Looking west towards Mortlake
and the Brewery.

A Heron catching crabs late one evening.

At certain times of the year, mainly late summer and early autumn, flocks of starlings can be seen swooping in spectacular fashion down onto the river to bathe and feed. Note the uniform way in which they have all landed on the rooftop.

Top: A panoramic view of the river from the top of The Bull's Head. I would like to thank the owners for giving me access to their home in order to take this picture.

A group fishing to check on fish stocks following some pollution back in the summer of 2011.

 # ROWING & THE BOAT RACE

Following the crews are a flotilla of boats, mainly judges and officials plus presumably some supporters.

The Oxford boat passing under Barnes Bridge and cruising to victory in spring 2011.

THE OXFORD AND CAMBRIDGE BOAT RACE

The race was the brainchild of two student friends in 1829 - Charles Merivale at Cambridge and Charles Wordsworth at Oxford. The first race took place on 12th March 1829 at Henley. Oxford were clear winners after a restart. The first race held on the Thames from Putney to Mortlake was rowed in 1845 and from 1856, apart from the war years, it became an annual event. During the nineteenth century spectators, not one of whom were known to have fallen into the river, hung from every vantage point high on Hammersmith Bridge hoping for a glimpse of the passing eights. Health and safety regulations prevent this happening today.

The race attracts thousands of spectators, with many displaying their colours.

Above: After the storm: rowing has to take part in all weathers, as powerfully demonstrated by this picture.

The Head of the
River Race is a timed
event and the crews
have to back up along
the river to start,
hence the queues.

The Head of the River Race: A timed race for eights, rowed annually on the
Thames from Mortlake to Putney. The first Head of the River Race took place on the
12th December 1926 with 40 crews competing. Today the entry is limited to 420
crews, several being crews from abroad who are strongly advised to take a practice run
on the extremely hazardous course before taking part in the race.

BARNES BRIDGE

The original slender, three-span cast iron bridge across the Thames designed by Joseph Locke, dates from the opening of the Hounslow loop line in 1849. In 1895 it was replaced by the more workmanlike crossing seen today. Designed by Edward Andrews for the London and South Western Railway Company its heavy wrought-iron bow string girders carrying two railway tracks across the river have caused it to be named by some as 'the ugliest bridge on the Thames'. I would tend to disagree with this sentiment, in fact I love it. Part of the original bridge survives unused on the up-stream side and the recent re-painting of the entire structure in two shades of grey, similar to the colours used on the 1849 bridge, have considerably improved its appearance. The bridge was listed as a Grade II structure in 1983.

Come and experience all
<u>this</u> on the Barnes Trail

There is much to celebrate about living in Barnes and early in the New Year of 2012 Barnes will be offering to share its beauty and uniqueness with the world, by inviting visitors to follow its very own trail. Barnes has been fortunate to win some inward investment from County Hall for this. The trail will be marked by metallic studs embedded in the surface of the walkways so that the route can easily be followed, in the same way that the Princess Diana Walk has been designed.

The walk will take in our village pond, the riverside, little alleyways, the Green, the Common and our shops, pubs and cafés. It will be a circular route of about 2kms and there will be extensions from it for the more adventurous. Points of interest whether they be historical, architectural or ecological will be described on informative plaques placed along the route. There will hopefully be a tourist information centre mid-way where a delightful map can be obtained (in the style of the map opposite) to provide further information and to keep as a reminder of a lovely day out.

The beautiful illustrations within the covers of this book will serve to remind you of just how much Barnes has to offer in terms of wildlife, Metropolitan Open Space, Georgian, Victorian and Edwardian architecture, historic churches, and a fascinating history. Whilst waiting for the trail to emerge, indulge yourself in the delights of this stunning little village haven so near to the noise and bustle of the capital city and yet so rural in its character. Enjoy these brilliantly displayed pictures from the comfort of your home and in the Spring, follow the trail, especially on launch day and invite your visitors thereafter to do the same.

Barnes Town Centre Manager

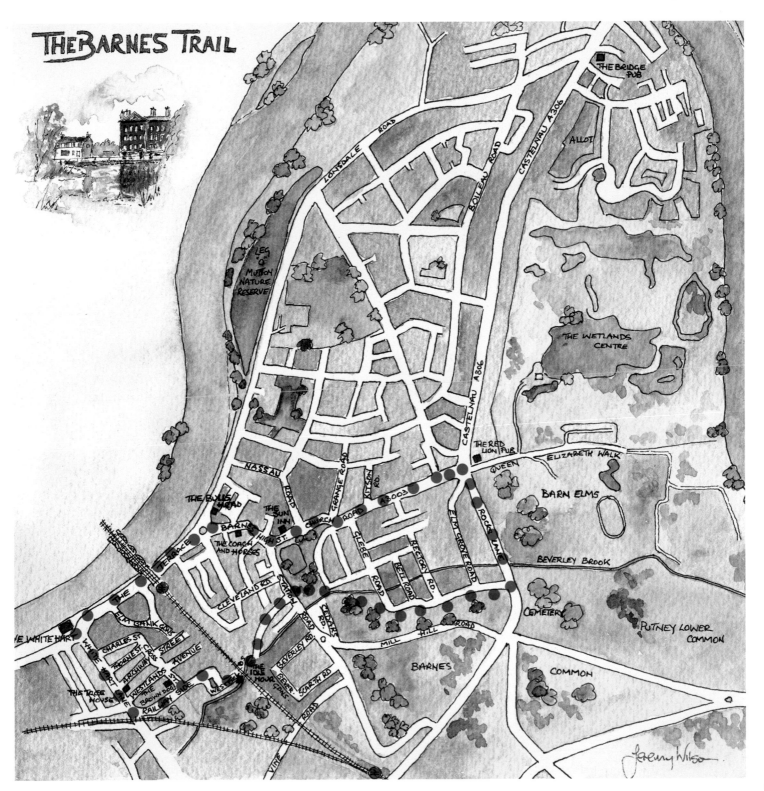

THE BARNES TRAIL

THE BRIDGE PUB

ALLOT

LONSDALE ROAD

BOILEAU ROAD

CASTELNAU A306

LEG "O" MUTTON NATURE RESERVE

THE WETLANDS CENTRE

CASTELNAU A306

THE RED LION PUB

QUEEN ELIZABETH WALK

NASSAU

BARN ELMS

THE BULLS HEAD

THE SUN INN

GRANGE ROAD

CHURCH ROAD

A3003

ELM GROVE ROAD

ROCKS LANE

BEVERLEY BROOK

BARNES HIGH ST.

THE COACH AND HORSES

GLEBE ROAD

RECTORY RD.

THE TERRACE

CLEVELAND RD.

STATION ROAD

BELL ROAD

CEMETERY

THE WHITE HART

ELM BANK GDNS

CHARLES ST.

THORNE ST.

ARCHWAY STREET

AVENUE

CEDARS RD.

BEVERLEY RD.

WESTLANDS

BEVER. GDNS.

SCARTH RD.

MILL HILL ROAD

PUTNEY LOWER COMMON

THE TREE HOUSE

WESTLANDS THE BROWN DOG

RAILWAY SIDE

THE IDLE HOUR

WEST

BARNES

COMMON

VINE ROAD

Jeremy Wilson

Purple Haze - Barnes Bridge - this is an original watercolour by Jeremy Wilson and produced exclusively for this book. A limited number of prints will be available after publication - please contact the publisher for more details.

STREET SCENES

Following a route that covers parts of the new Barnes Trail, I have tried to give you a flavour of Barnes street life and some of the places along the way. In doing so, I hope that I have helped you experience some places for the first time. So starting at the station we travel down Station Road, through the High Street, along The Terrace and through West Barnes over to Rocks Lane, taking in the Vine Road area. We then return to The Pond along Church Road before striking out for North Barnes via Castelnau, finally returning to the centre via Lonsdale Road.

Church Road

The railway that did so much to
change Barnes back in the 19th century.

The path to Barnes Station from
the Upper Richmond Road
junction with Rocks Lane, which
can be seen in the distance.

All pictures are of Barnes Station except the one on the right, which is of Barnes Bridge Station's eastbound platform.

The Tudor-style brick-built station, opened on 27th July 1946 when the line to Richmond was built. It is the only survivor of others on the line built in the same style by Sir William Tite. Barnes became a junction station when the first section of the Hounslow Loop Line opened on 22nd August 1849. The station and all lines serving it are today operated by South West Trains. The Grade II listed station house survives, but is now privately owned and no longer part of the railway.

From the Station, you follow Station Road towards Barnes Village, passing Scarth and Mill Hill Roads.
Top right and left: Scarth Road.
Top left: Mill Hill Road.

Top left and bottom right: A relatively new development reflected in Beverley Brook. **Top right:** Joy McDonald's shop of mirrors. **Right:** Footpath from the common to the station, connecting Mill Hill Road and Station Road.

Left: The cherry trees in blossom on the island by the pond, where Station Road meets the High Street.
Opposite: The Pond and High Street taken from the top of the red building in the picture below.
Below: The Sun Inn winter 2010, before they painted it blue in the spring of 2011.

Farmers' Market: Every Saturday in the car park of Essex House doctors' surgery, opposite the pond, there is a Farmers' Market, where you can find all kinds of wholesome foods.

Thought to date from the 18th century, but possibly a little earlier, **The Sun Inn** was sometimes recorded as The Sun Coffee House. Its unrivalled venue with outdoor seating facing Barnes Pond attracts customers from a wide area in all seasons, but especially during the summer months. The gap to the left once led to the workshop & premises of the village wheelwright and blacksmith's forge. Left of the gap are two houses built in 1854 and advertised as 'ornate villas'. They replaced a substantial Elizabethan E' shaped property, known as The Mansion House. One wing survived demolition and is now Membery's Childrenswear Shop, seen further to the left (see the next page).

Picture bottom left: The Flower Stall, which can be found in the entrance to The Sun Inn's car park.
Right: One of the regular markets held beside the pond.

The Barnes Bowling Club: Hidden from view at the rear of the Sun Inn Car Park is a private Crown Bowling Green, beautifully maintained and belonging to the Barnes Bowling Club. Crown Bowls, well known in the north of England but rare in the south, is played diagonally across the green. The Green dates from c1795, since when it has remained in continuous use.

Looking west towards the river.

Top: Rose House was once thought to date from the 19thC but when threatened with demolition in 1972 the house was found to date from 1632 when it was an inn named The Sign of the Rose. Strong local protests resulted in a public inquiry where documentary evidence given by the Barnes and Mortlake History Society and the results of a survey by the GLC Historic Buildings Inspector, ensured its survival. In 1974 it was bought by the Barnes Community Association since when it has been their H.Q.

This street of small shops and businesses at the heart of Barnes Village, is thought to have originated as the pathway between the two great open fields of medieval Barnes, the Northfield and the Westonfield, or Westfield. It led from the village settlement around the Green to the river docking place, named as *le new docke* in 1400. A past local historian suggested that the pronounced bend in the High Street may have been trodden into being by the feet of men and draught animals having to avoid an immovable obstruction such as a large boulder or tree root in their path.

Below: Looking west towards the river.
Below right: Looking east towards the pond.

Much prized by locals for the quality of its meat, **Seal's** is probably the oldest established business in Barnes. In the nineteenth century it occupied both its current premises and the shop next door on the corner of Stanton Road. Back then there were fields behind the shop and cattle were brought in and slaughtered on the premises. Above the façade was a Royal Coat of Arms awarded by Queen Victoria for supplying joints of beef to White Lodge in Richmond Park when Her Majesty was in residence.

Far Left: The Coach and Horses pub in the High Street dates from the eighteenth century and is very deceptive in that it is much larger than you think, with a garden stretching far back from the road.

Left and below: The area behind Café Nero on the High Street.

Left: Barnes is lucky enough to have lots of individual specialist shops, like The Fish Shop.

One of many Barnes visitors, this cheeky little Goldfinch was spotted up on the rooftops.

As the High Street meets The Terrace and the River, you find The Bull's Head, which can trace its history back almost 400 years. Starting out as The Sign of the Rayne Deer, it became The Bull's Head in 1735. Since 1952 it has been a mecca for all lovers of Jazz, with live performances every night.

WHITE HART LANE AND WEST BARNES

From The Terrace, you move into the area of Barnes dominated by White Hart Lane. On the roundabout where White Hart Lane meets the junction of The Terrace and Mortlake High Street you find Ye White Hart pub (see left and over the page), several popular cafés with outside seating and a Sainsbury's Local (see opposite).

Starting out as the King's Arms, it changed to Ye White Hart in the eighteenth century. Rebuilt several times, the present large house dates from 1899. Always popular with rowers, the White Hart's commanding position on the riverside just above Barnes Bridge has for many years been a favourite viewing point for The Boat Race.

Although officially in Mortlake, shops on the west side of White Hart Lane and such places as The Depot are still very much part of the Barnes community. The Depot, above and top right, is a fashionable bar and restaurant.

Right: Annie's Restaurant, which can be found half way up White Hart Lane is another popular venue.

Top page opposite: White Hart Lane is carved in half by the railway and locals have to suffer being regularly caught out by the level crossing.

Bottom page opposite and right: White Hart Lane is quite long and has a lively parade of shops, interspersed with residential homes.

Above Top: The Treehouse Pub and Restaurant is another popular haunt, which until very recently had an excellent function room. In October 2011 they had the bad luck to suffer a fire in their upstairs room; thankfully no one was hurt and hopefully it will not be too long until they have this up and running again.

WESTFIELDS ALLOTMENTS

These allotments placed on undeveloped land between the railway and the pretty cottages in Railway Side are a rare survival from one of the two great open fields of Barnes, the Westfield. The allotment holders who tend their crops today, might sometimes give a thought to the Barnes peasants doing much the same in the early medieval period on the same plot of land. They might also think about the market garden labourers gathering the produce of the field for the London market from the 17th to the late 19th century.

Priests Bridge and The Halfway House: This is
the boundary between Barnes and Mortlake and where
Beverley Brook goes under the Upper Richmond Road.
Until the turn of the century, the Upper Richmond
Road had not been diverted and so Priests Bridge was
part of the main road.

Left: The Brown Dog pub and restaurant can be found tucked away in Cross Street - see also page 152

Above: Another frequented pub and restaurant in this part of Barnes is The Idle Hour, which is tucked away amongst the many footpaths that you find here.
Left: The pretty little cottages of Railway Side.

As the picture above clearly states, **Barnes Primary School** was founded in 1903 as Barnes Infant School. You can just make out the modern facilities through the gates, as the school has in the last ten years been upgraded and new buildings introduced. A bit of a shame but they no longer use this entrance, probably on account of the need for greater security. The school is large with buildings either side of Railway Side.

This Page: St Michael and All Angels, Elm Bank Gardens. St. Michael's began in 1877 as a school church housed in a small temporary building. It was intended to serve the growing population in the narrowstreets of terraced cottages rising rapidly on the former market gardens of the Westfield. The new church, designed by architect Charles Innes, was completed and consecrated in 1893. Initially served by the clergy of the Parish Church, St.Michael and All Angels was declared a separate parish in 1919.

This Page Top: The view of Vine Road from the cricket pitch.
Above and Right: Vine Road.

Below: As with White Hart Lane, Vine Road is dominated by a railway crossing but unlike it, Vine Road has two, so double the trouble.

Above and Below: Beverley Walk.

The other pictures on this page are a collection of shots taken of the myriad of paths to be found in this part of Barnes.

Far left and left: Long Walk

VINE ROAD
RECREATION GROUND

Vine Road Recreation Ground was in old times part of the large Westfield, then becoming an orchard before finally being turned into a park in the 1920's.

Above and left: Spring blossoms in **Elm Grove Road** are a yearly delight to the eye. The road was laid out on the site of Elm Grove, one of the lost houses of Barnes demolished in 1896. The house stood within the borders of the Barn Elms estate near to the present day HSBC bank, with grounds extending beyond the Beverley Brook to Barnes Common. It has been identified as the house occupied from 1703 by Jacob Tonson (1656-1736), who was a stationer, publisher and secretary to the Kit-Cat Club. Its members were the leading Whigs of the day, and are said to have met at the house with the purpose of promoting the House of Hanover and the Protestant Succession.

Top left and left:
Beverley Brook as it meanders between the houses that are bordered by Glebe Road and Rocks Lane.

ROCKS LANE

From Vine Road you cross the
Common to Rocks Lane.

Rocks Lane is bordered on one side by a row of
houses and on the other by a majestic line of Plane
trees and part of the Barn Elms playing fields.

Far left and top:
The top of Rocks Lane as it meets Castelnau.
Left: Rocks Lane Plane trees seen looking north up the cycle path.

Right: The Nonsuch shop on the corner of Castelnau and Church Street.

This page top and right: The Red Lion, Castelnau. First recorded in 1718, when there was nothing to be seen to the north but farmland, this well-known pub was, at that time, a thatched hostelry known as The Strugglers. Destroyed by fire in 1835 it was rebuilt shortly after and re-named The Red Lion. During the 1880's it was a popular meeting place for the many Cycling Clubs in south-west London who stopped for tea and a game at the skittle alley.

This page: The Church Road shops at the top of Castelnau opposite The Red Lion, including Riva, the award winning Italian restaurant.

Bottom of the opposite page:

Byfeld Hall, opened on 20th December 1906, was built on the site of a demolished private residence, Byfield House. The building was made up of two halls, one large and one small; the larger of the two could be hired for amateur theatricals, concerts or dances, the smaller for private events such as whist drives and parties. From 1910 until 1925 it operated as a cinema under a variety of names. Its most illustrious, albeit brief period, began in 1925 when Phillip Ridgeway, a budding impressario, opened it as an art-house theatre. Famous names from the past, such as Charles Laughton, John Gielgud, Robert Newton and Claude Rains trod the boards in a series of productions, but a lack of funds resulted in closure after barely a year, when it once again became a cinema. In 1952 it became a studio for television commercials and later a recording studio where hits by The Beatles, The Rolling Stones, Pink Floyd, Led Zeppelin, Sting, U2 and many other leading groups were recorded. Having recently been sold by the beleaguered EMI, current plans are for the site to return to being an independent cinema with other attractions.

Sonny's Restaurant and Bar.

THE PARISH CHURCH OF ST. MARY, BARNES

The church dates from c1100. A major fire on June 8th1978 left little standing Fortunately, the south and east walls of the 12th /13th century chapel and the tower, c1485, survived to become an integral part of the rebuilt church designed by prize-winning architect Edward Cullinan. The re-hallowing of the new church took place on 26th February1984.

The church tower from the gardens of Strawberry House.

The church from Church Road.

This page: The view from the top of St Mary's Church Tower, which is traditionally open to the public in exchange for a small fee on the occasion of Barnes Fair (see page 32). **Top and above:** The view of Barnes looking east.
Bottom Left: Barnes Bookshop.

Top left: The shops in Church Road.
Top Right: The view of the junction of Church Road, Castelnau, Queen Elizabeth Walk and Rocks Lane.
Left: The Chez Moi Chez Vous Café & Epicerie at Karavan, which can be found down the little alleyway opposite The Olympic Cinema. A haven on a fine day, where you can sit outside.

Left: The Homestead, Church Road. Built in the reign of Queen Anne (1702-1714) this attractive house with its old walled forecourt is one of the finest period houses remaining in Barnes. Seen together with its neighbours, St. Mary's Church and Strawberry House, it presents a perfect picture of a bygone age.

Above: Kitson Hall, Kitson Road.

Above: Strawberry House, Church Road. The former Barnes Rectory lost a substantial part of its land when Kitson Road, named after the Rector, Benjamin Meredyth Kitson, was constructed in 1907. A further plot was used for the Church Hall in 1927, Kitson Hall. Built on the site of an earlier house, c1717, it ceased to be the Rectory in 1939 and stayed empty for some years until being finally sold in 1955, since when it has been a private residence. I am grateful to the current owner for allowing me to take an up-to-date picture.

Church Road shops, including Two Peas in a Pod, with their distinctive bike outside. **Right:** The bench that looks out on Glebe Road, where the doctors' surgery is just up on the left.

St Osmund's Primary
School in Church
Road is behind the
white house.

The Grange, the house
on the corner of Grange
Road and Church Road.

Almost next door to the award winning local newsagent, Natson's, a
new Greek restaurant is due to open soon.

St Osmund's Catholic Primary School:

St Osmund's occupies a much larger space than you would first gather by merely looking from the road. It extends quite far back - room for over 400 children in their care. The school began as a convent school at the the turn of the last century and St Osmund's took over in 1969.

This page: Church Road from a variety of angles.

In addition to the two plaques on The Terrace, there is also this one to one of our finest composers, Herbert Howells that can be found behind the Green in Beverley Close.

Left and above: This is the side view of one of four houses, Nos. 31-37, once known locally as Atwell's Folly. Professor Henry Atwell, one-time tutor to the Crown Prince of the Royal Dutch House of Orange-Nassau, ran a boarding school for boys in a house on the site from 1859, naming it Nassau House School. When he retired in 1890 the house was replaced by the four houses. They were built close to the road with basements, regarded by the locals as foolhardy in an area prone to flooding, hence the nickname. Nassau Road was laid out on the grounds of the school from which it took its name.

Top: An impressive wall on one of the houses down Castelnau.
Above: Barnes Library.
Left: A Cyclist travelling north on Castelnau.

NORTH BARNES

CASTELNAU VILLAS. After the opening of the first Hammersmith Bridge in 1827, it was some time before the first of the ribbon development of houses began to replace the market gardens and farmlands stretching back from the newly built approach road, Upper Bridge Road, (now Castelnau). Castelnau Villas were the first to be built in 1842, six years into the reign of Queen Victoria. The architect was Henry Laxton. Originally un-numbered, they are now Nos. 84-122 and 91-125 Castelnau.

St. Osmund's Church, the first purpose built Roman Catholic Church in Barnes, opened in 1954. From the end of the nineteenth century Mass had been ministered by a priest from Mortlake in the chapel of a girls' school in Church Road, Barnes which later became part of St. Osmund's R.C. School. In 1908 the congregation bought No. 77 Castelnau, which served as a temporary chapel and housing for the Priest. This later became the site for the present church, the opening being much delayed by WW2. No. 79 seen to the right of the church is the Presbytery or Priest's House.

Top and Right: Holy Trinity Church, Castelnau, built in 1868 on the east side of Upper Bridge Road (re-named Castelnau, 1889) Holy Trinity replaced an earlier chapel-of-ease built in 1851 for the growing community in North Barnes. Originally served by clergy from St. Mary's Parish Church, Holy Trinity became a separate parish in 1880. The architect, Thomas Allom, lived in Lonsdale Road. **Above Left:** Shops on the east side of Castelnau as the road approaches Hammersmith Bridge.

Tesco Express.

The Bridge Pub and Gardens started life as the Bridge Hotel in 1866.

The west side shops on Castelnau
and the approach to Hammersmith
Bridge.

Below and left - Castelnau Estate: This pleasant well-laid out cottage style estate of 640 ferro-concrete houses was built in 1926. It was built on Harold Bessant's market garden land by Henry Boot & Sons by a method known as the Boot Pier and Panel System. Owned by the London County Council, it was part of a scheme to ease the overcrowded conditions in Fulham & Hammersmith. Richmond upon Thames Council bought the estate in 1971. During the late 70s several tenants bought their homes under the Central Government's 'right to buy scheme'. In November 1983 reports that identical Boot Houses in other parts of the country had been declared structurally unsound, resulted in several owner-occupied homes on the Castelnau Estate being virtually rebuilt in conventional red brick. It was later found that all but one of the houses on the estate were in fact perfectly sound.

Above: Junction of Stillingfleet Road and Barnes Avenue.
Left: Hammersmith Bridge.

Lowther Primary School: With the development of the Castelnau Estate in 1926, there was a need for a new school and within three years Lowther Primary started in Stillingfleet Road. They have a magnificent main building, which reflects the age it was built in and are currently undergoing considerable investment, with new buildings in the process of being added. They have a lot of space and put it to good use, with an allotment and even some chickens.

Castelnau Recreation Ground:
Tucked away behind Washington Road and Barnes Avenue, this is a great open space. The Council consulted the residents regarding the gate and the result is rather magnificent.

The present **Hammersmith Bridge**, designed by Sir Joseph William Bazalgette, was opened by Prince Albert Victor of Wales on Saturday 18th June 1887. It replaced an earlier bridge, designed by William Tierney Clark and opened without ceremony in October 1827. By 1877 the narrow width of Tierney Clark's bridge and its safety under increasingly heavy traffic was in question and in 1882 the bridge committee voted in favour of a new bridge. A temporary bridge was erected on clusters of timber piles close to the western side of the old bridge during the period of demolition and construction. This was removed shortly after the opening of the new bridge in 1887.

How about this for a Pumpkin - room for a small gardener inside!

Barn Elms Allotment, North Barnes. This has to be one of the smartest looking allotments you'll find; it has manicured grass pathways betwen each plot and it has its own highway with a speed limit. It is home to some lovely people, who clearly care passionately about what they do.

Right: Lynda and her wonderful hat.
Top: Queenie and Hayley - they even had the smartest looking shed you'll ever see too!

Page opposite, above and top right:
The view west from Hammersmith Bridge.
Right: Harrods Depository from the river.
Top left: The temple and fountain that greets visitors to Harrods Village and Barnes Waterside.

Harrods Village and Barnes Waterside:
Top, left and right: The Pond.
Far right: The very distinctive apartment blocks within Barnes Waterside.

ST PAUL'S SCHOOL & COLET COURT

This famous public school for boys was founded in 1509 by the Dean of St. Paul's Cathedral, John Colet. In 1884 it moved from its original site near the Cathedral to West Kensington where it remained until, together with its preparatory school, Colet Court, it moved to Barnes in 1968. The new school with sports grounds and a boathouse by the Thames was purpose built on a disused reservoir site.

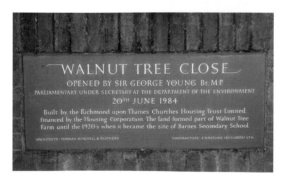

WALNUT TREE CLOSE
OPENED BY SIR GEORGE YOUNG Bt.M.P.
PARLIAMENTARY UNDER SECRETARY AT THE DEPARTMENT OF THE ENVIRONMENT
20TH JUNE 1984
Built by the Richmond upon Thames Churches Housing Trust Limited,
financed by the Housing Corporation. The land formed part of Walnut Tree
Farm until the 1920's when it became the site of Barnes Secondary School.
ARCHITECTS: THOMAS MITCHELL & PARTNERS   CONTRACTORS: E. GOSTLING (BUILDERS) LTD.

Top and far left: Suffolk Road Recreation Ground.

Left: The convenience store at the bottom of Verdun Road as it meets Lonsdale Road.

Bottom Left: The Plaque in Walnut Tree Close, off Lonsdale Road, marking the site of Walnut Tree Farm and the old Barnes Secondary School. The Farm was sold in 1925 and the school built in its place.

Below, right and far right. The Swedish School, Lonsdale Road.

Above and Right. An example of the impressive villas to be found along the top of Lonsdale Road as it nears Hammersmith Bridge.

HARRODIAN SCHOOL

An independent pre-prep and preparatory school for boys and girls opened in 1993 in Lonsdale Road. Originally occupying the former house and sports club belonging to the department store, Harrods of Knightsbridge, it has since been considerably enlarged and currently has around 900 pupils.

Top left and right:
Small Profit Dock.
Above and left:
Barnes Sports Club,
which can be found
opposite Small Profit
Dock on Lonsdale
Road. Besides cricket,
amongst the other
sports played are
tennis and squash.

Above: Small Profit Dock is the name that has been given to the small triangular stretch of land off Lonsdale Road and opposite Gerard and Nassau Roads. The actual dock is the curved railing on the embankment by the river. The parking bay at Small Profit Dock has been renovated since this picture was taken. The other three pictures are of Ring-Necked Parakeets fighting over the hole in the tree that can be found in the centre of the dock.

HIDDEN BARNES

Left: From a large set of signs to be found in the beer garden of The Brown Dog, Cross Street, in West Barnes.

Above: The Garages to be found behind the houses on Charles Street, West Barnes.

IN RESPECTFUL MEMORY OF

MARC BOLAN
30th SEPTEMBER 1947
16th SEPTEMBER 1977

MUSICIAN, WRITER, POET

DONATED BY PERFORMING RIGHT SOCIETY
IN RECOGNITION OF HIS OUTSTANDING
CONTRIBUTION TO BRITISH MUSIC

Above: Nasa comes to Barnes in the form of this spaceman, on the veranda of a house on the corner of Gerard Road and Lonsdale Road.

Above right and right: The place in Queen's Ride that the singer Marc Bolan had his unfortunate accident back in the 70's plus one of the many tributes to be found there.

The effigies on the houses above are quite unique. The builder of these houses on the north side of Cedars Road finished them in 1901, which coincided with the ending of the Boer War and it is thought that he decided to date them by including two heroes from the war (Earl Kitchener and Earl Roberts above) and Edward VII and his wife Queen Alexandra, top, as Edward became King that year.

Above & Right:
A couple of fun weather vanes, above, Lonsdale Road and right, Nassau Road.

Above: The rather nasty looking skull, to be found up on the wall on the right of St Mary's Church main door.

Right:
The alleyway that runs between Berkeley Road and Ferry Road. Owned by the Church, people are allowed to use it, but are asked to treat it with respect.

Middle above: Thorne Passage: This ancient track way ran due south-east across the Westfield as it does today, beginning at the junction of White Hart Lane and Barnes Terrace. In times past it provided a convenient dry route from Mortlake to Barnes when the river was in flood.

Above: The small shops and offices to be found behind the main shops at the top of Church Road, at the entrance of Bracken Gardens.

Red Terrace - Barnes - this is an original watercolour by Jeremy Wilson and produced exclusively for this book.
A limited number of prints will be available after publication - please contact the publisher for more details.

154

OPEN SPACES

We are fortunate that living in Barnes we are surrounded by some glorious stretches of open space, from Barnes Common to the Leg o' Mutton Nature Reserve and The London Wetand Centre.

Barnes Common

Large Skipper
butterfly.

BARNES COMMON

The common covers over 100 acres and is a designated Local Nature Reserve. Owned by the Church since the Middle Ages, the Common is managed by the Local Authority (Richmond-upon-Thames), which is advised and assisted by the Friends of Barnes Common, who you will regularly see out with their mowers and gardening equipment (see page 167). Of special note are the areas of acid grassland, which are rare in London and characterised by where the soil is thin and sandy. A lot of work has been done recently by the FOBC to try and maintain the growth of the scrub in order to protect the grassy areas.

Above: The houses in the middle of the common and an area referred to as Mill Hill, although the mill has long gone.
Left: The cricket pitch by the railway line.
Top: The footbal pitch.
Top Left: Plane tree seeds.

Top: The common beside Barnes Green and Beverley Brook.
Above: The path to Priory Lane from the station.
Right: Common Road.

Cricket pitch beside the station:

Top left opposite page: After a storm.

Below: After a particulary windy period the fencing around the cricket pitch was blown over and the resident Kestrel lost some of his landing posts.

Bottom: Blackthorn blossom is very beautiful in spring but is over very quickly and loses its brilliant white colour.

One night a week in the summer, the local cricket club who use this ground have an evening match, creating some long shadows as the sun sets.

Top and above: Besides the Horse Chestnut on the Green that has recently been cut back (see page 26), this tree was cut down earlier in 2011 on account of the damage being caused by the mining moth. Sadly, one or two of the others surrounding the pitch also look in a bad way - with the tell-tale signs in the leaves (top left). **Top right:** A green woodpecker hides away amongst the leaves. **Left:** Shadows across the path that leads to the station from Queens Ride.

We are lucky to have on the common many different types of butterfly, some of which are featured here.

Top Left: Speckled Wood
Top Right: Large White
Above: Meadow Brown
Centre Right: Purple Hairstreak
Right: Small Copper

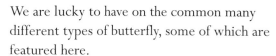

Top left: Small Heath **Top right:** Small Copper
Above: Gatekeeper **Above right:** Comma

Top: The common in spring beside Beverley Brook and the new reedbed.
Above: The football pitch in spring.

Above: Plane tree seeds set against the late setting sun.
Left: The path away from the station, across the common towards Mill Hill, with beautiful purple Honesty flowering around the wooden stumps.

Top and middle: The volunteers from the Friends of Barnes Common cutting the grass.
Above: An artist enjoying the view.

Top: It was very dry for the first few months of 2011 and the common became extremely parched, as if it was July.
Above: A Broad Bodied Chaser Dragonfly **Above right:** A family of Green Woodpeckers silhouetted against the sky.

Top: The view east across the common towards the houses on Ranelagh Avenue. **Above:** Broom flowering in spring.
Above left: The path east across the common towards Mill Hill and Rocks Lane.

Opposite Page: A fantastic cloud display over the common near Mill Hill.
Bottom Left: Beverley Brook near the bridge to the Green.
BottomRight: The path from the Lower Richmond Road towards Rocks Lane.

Top and above: A fox enjoys itself lying in the sun on the patch of rough ground down by the railway line. It's an excellent place for wildlife. However, in late 2011 men were working on the station and had to clear part of this patch of common.

Left: Feeding time for this young Great Spotted Woodpecker.

Above: It's wonderful how nature and sport come together so well on Barn Elms.

Barn Elms:
Top: The view across to Barn Elms from the field beside Rocks Lane Sports Centre.
Bottom left & middle: The Barn Elms Plane is the oldest in London and can be seen in the top picture; it is the tallest tree poking out from the wood.

Above: The back of the Rocks Lane Multi Sports Centre's sports pavilion and the field beside it used by footballers and dog walkers alike.

Top: Dawn across Barn Elms one frosty spring morning.
Left: This cricket match had some unusual spectators.

Top: The private fishing lake owned by the local fishing club, next to the car park off Queen Elizabeth Walk. Thank you to the members of The Barnes and Mortlake Angling Society for allowing me in to take these pictures.

Right: A pair of Herons regularly nest in a tree beside the lake. Perhaps not exactly what the members would like, as presumably they are competition, but they seem quite proud of them.

Above and top: The playground at Rocks Lane Multi Sports Centre.
Above right: The disused public lavatory facing onto Rocks Lane stands on what was named the Little Long Croft. At the back there are some changing and shower facilities.
Opposite Page: The field featured bottom and top left, off Rocks Lane, is a surviving medieval meadow once known as the Town Croft or Great Long Croft. **Middle:** Rocks Lane Multi Sports Centre.
Middle Right: The lane off Rocks Lane that leads to a small car park, Barnes Common and Barnes Old Cemetery (see next page).

THE OLD BARNES CEMETERY On Barnes Common, beside Rocks Lane Sports Centre

Below: The grave of the Attwell Family.

Above: The impressive Hedgmen Memorial.

Known today as Barnes Old Cemetery or Rocks Lane Cemetery, this small burial ground on 2 acres of land within Barnes Common, opened in 1854, shortly after the churchyard of the Parish Church of St. Mary was closed for burials. Some 3,000 burials took place here, the majority being of local people, before it was declared full and closed in the mid-1950s. Since its closure the majority of the gravestones have been vandalised, lending an air of dereliction to the once pleasant surroundings. Recent efforts by the Friends of Barnes Common have vastly improved the general ambience and in 1980 the Managers, Richmond Council, succeeded in having the Cemetery declared a Local Nature Reserve. **Above right:** This is the grave of Ebenezer Cobb Morley, who lived locally and is famous for having devised the first rules for The Football Association. There is some talk about improving the graveyard in time for the FA's 150th anniversary in 2013 in honour of Cobb Morley and its other illustrious inhabitants.

BENCHES   do *you* have a favourite?

Small Profit Dock

The bench near the Emanuel School boat house overlooking the Terrace and Barnes Bridge.

Looking West over Vine Road Recreation Ground.

The Green

The Pond

Not doing so well, by the crossroads on the common opposite Mill Hill on Rocks Lane.

On the common by the footpath that leads from Mill Hill to Ranelagh Avenue.

The Green - by the bridge over Beverley Brook

The Leg o'Mutton

On the Towpath by Ye White Hart

The football pitch by the station

Small Profit Dock

Railway Side, Westfields

Barnes Waterside, North Barnes

Barnes Sports Club

The cricket pitch by the station

The common near Mill Hill

Top and above: The lake looking west.

THE LEG O' MUTTON NATURE RESERVE

In Barnes we are thoroughly spoilt in being surrounded by plenty of green and open spaces and this is a particular favourite. Originally a reservoir, in 1990 Richmond Council recognised its importance and made it one of their Local Nature Reserves, lending it status and long term protection. It gets its name from the distinctive shape of the lake and is a haven for a great variety of wildlife. If you have never visited you are in for a treat. It's a hidden gem, concealed between Lonsdale Road and the river.

The Mallard ducks even climb amongst the trees here.

186

The changing seasons - opposite page, autumn and winter and this page, early spring.

Top left: Ducks enjoying the use of the floating rafts placed there for that very reason. The black and white ones are Tufted Ducks and the red headed ones are Pochards.

Top right and above: A Grey Heron

Middle left and left: An unusual combination for this Mallard, one white duckling and one the normal colour.

Top left: Egyptian Geese are known for nesting in amongst the trees. Here it has been joined by a crow who is obviously worrying the goose.

Top right, right and above: A pair of Tawny Owls regularly nest in the hole featured above, although I'm not altogether sure they were successful parents in 2011 and let's hope for better things in 2012.

Giant Hogweed shot against a backdrop of the lake.

The path around the lake in early spring, on the Lonsdale Road side.

It's not surprising finding painters enjoying the scenery, as there is plenty of inspiration.

The resident pair of Mute Swans were again successful parents in 2011. This must be in part because of the rafts that have been placed on the lake, as this ensures that when young, the cygnets have somewhere safe to go.

Below: I am not sure exactly what it was that was attracting these flies but there were a lot of them.

The view of The Leg of Mutton from across the Thames in Dukes Meadows. They have recently improved the view by cutting back the trees alongside the river.

THE WWT LONDON WETLAND CENTRE

The Wetland Centre opened in 2000 and is a brilliant example of where commerce and nature can come together and both sides win. The centre was formed from four disused reservoirs. Thames Water, who owned the land, came together with Berkeley Homes and The Wildlife and Wetlands Trust to form what is now a world renowned site for nature.

Above: Female Mallard duck
Left: White-faced Whistling ducks

Top: Mute swan
Left: The Peacock viewing tower, in the centre of the reserve, offering fantastic views across the complete area. **Above:** Mallard duck family

The new Berkeley bat house.

The statue to Sir Peter Scott outside the main building.

"When I came to live here twenty-five years ago, on behalf of the Barn Elms Protection Association I went to visit Sir Peter Scott at Slimbridge on the Severn Estuary to discuss the idea of bringing a wildfowl and wetlands to Barn Elms. He leapt at the idea and told me, "If the birds like it in Barnes they'll come. If they really like it, they'll come again and again". Birds are fine judges of a place. The London Wetland Centre is now the finest urban wildlife site in Europe. The Berwick swans have spoken. Enough said."

Gyles Brandreth, autumn 2011 - local resident, broadcaster, writer and many things besides.

Little Creasted Grebes

Below: Mute swans can be extremely territorial and chase off any intruders.